Name: _____

Why did the mouse want a pair of nail scissors?

What will the mouse need if he wants to take a nap?

Name:

Answer the questions below using complete sentences.

Name some things asked for by the mouse.

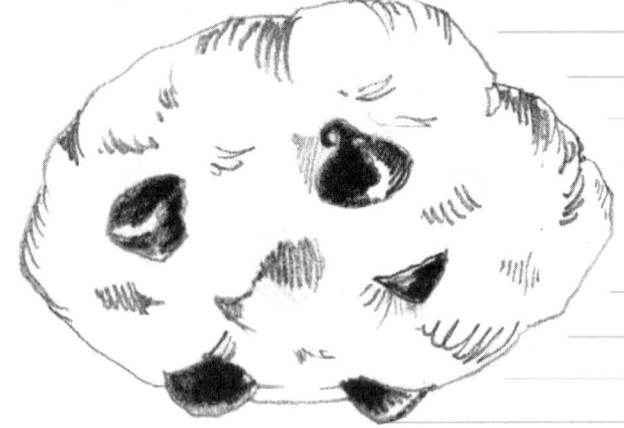

Why did the mouse want a mirror?

Name: _____

Fill in the blanks with the missing words.

If you give a mouse a _____, he's going to ask for a glass of _____. When you give him the _____, he'll probably ask for a _____. When he's finished, he'll ask for a _____. Then he'll want to look in a _____, to make sure he doesn't have a milk _____. When he looks into the _____, he might notice his _____ needs a trim. So he'll probably ask for a pair of nail _____. When he is finished giving himself a _____, he'll want a _____ to sweep up. He'll start _____. He might get carried away and sweep every _____ in the house. He may even end up washing the _____ as well! When he is done, he'll probably want to take a

Fill in the blanks, continued.

You'll have to fix up a little _____ for him with a _____ and a _____. He'll crawl in, make himself comfortable and fluff the _____ a few times. He'll probably ask you to read him a _____. So you'll read to him from one of your _____ and he'll ask to see the _____. When he looks at the _____, he'll get so excited he'll want to draw one of his own. He'll ask for _____ and _____. He'll draw a _____. When the _____ is finished, he'll want to sign his _____ with a _____.

Name:

My favorite kind of cookies are

Write at least three sentences describing your favorite kind of cookies. Include why you like them best.

Name:

Take a trip to your local pet store and make a book of your observations of a mouse. Photocopy the artwork below onto card stock, then cut out the strip and fold along the dotted lines like an accordion. The extra strip can be glued on the end for a longer book.

My Little Mouse Book	*Color:*	*Size:*	*Favorite feature:*	*Tail length:*

Name:

Fill in the blanks, continued.

Then he'll want to hang his picture on your _____. Which means he'll need _____. He'll hang up his _____ and stand back and look at it. Looking at the _____ will remind him that he's _____. So... he'll ask for a glass of _____. And chances are if he asks for a glass of _____ he's going to want a _____ to go with it.

Name: _____

Draw the picture that the mouse might have drawn.

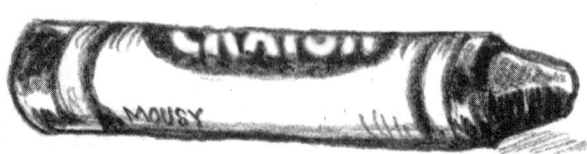

Name:

My favorite kind of cookies are

Write at least three sentences describing your favorite kind of cookies. Include why you like them best.

first favorites
COMPREHENSION GUIDE
VOLUME ONE

Comprehension Questions
by Laurie Detweiler

Illustration and Design
by Ned Bustard

www.VeritasPress.com
(800) 922-5082

First Edition 2002

Copyright ©2002 Veritas Press
www.VeritasPress.com
(800) 922-5082

ISBN 1-930710-62-3

All rights reserved. Permission is granted to make unlimited photocopies of this entire manual for the school or homeschool that purchased this manual. Otherwise, no part of this book may be reproduced without permission from Veritas Press, except by a reviewer who may quote brief passages in a review; nor may any part of this book be reproduced, stored in a retrieval system or transmitted in any form by any means, electronic, mechanical, photocopying, recording or otherwise, without prior permission from Veritas Press.

Printed in the United States of America.

First Favorites Comprehension Guide
Table of Contents

How to Use this Guide 5
Curious George 7–16
Caps for Sale 17–22
Corduroy 23–30
If You Give a Mouse a Cookie 31–42
Blueberries for Sal 43–52
The Little Engine that Could 53–60
Floss 61–70
A Chair for My Mother 71–82
Harry the Dirty Dog 83–90
Billy and Blaze 91–100
Bread and Jam for Frances 101–110
Doctor DeSoto 111–124
Frog and Toad are Friends 125–144
Frog and Toad All Year
Answers 145–148

FIRST FAVORITES COMPREHENSION GUIDE
How to Use this Guide

What is *First Favorites*? It is a collection of literature guides to assist beginning readers to enjoy and comprehend a book. Once children learn how to decode words they need to learn how to engage the materials. They need to learn how to comprehend what they are reading. So how do we do this?

The books may be read in any order, but we have placed them in order based on difficulty. Generally, we spend three to four days per book. With chapter books such as *Frog and Toad are Friends* you may need five to seven days. Children generally will read the book twice during this time. They should be reading the books aloud with you. You should help them to decode unfamiliar words. Be sure to let children sound out the words, rather than just giving them the pronunciation. Teach them to read with expression, which includes following the punctuation.

The comprehension questions and activities are there to help children focus on particular portions of the text and to help you assess their understanding of it. The children should be allowed to refer back to the text if needed. Although the answers in the guide are provided in incomplete sentences, you should expect the student to answer in complete sentences.

Example:
Question: Who was Floss?
Answer: Floss was a Border Collie.

The art activities are meant to bring the text alive. Children always retain more when they work with the material. Handwriting exercises will provide students practice sentences to rehearse manuscript writing.

Below you will see four icons. Each will help you identify how to use each worksheet.

COMPREHENSION QUESTIONS, WRITING EXERCISES

COMPREHENSION ACTIVITIES, WRITING EXERCISES

ART ACTIVITIES

HANDWRITING EXERCISES

Enjoy! Curl up with a good book and read the day away. It is our desire that your students will become life long readers and look back on these years with great delight.

Sincerely,

Merlin Detweiler
Laurie Detweiler

CURIOUS GEORGE

BY H.A. REY

Name: _____

After reading the book Curious George, *(circle) the answer that best fills in the blank.*

Curious George was a _____.
man   dog   monkey

Curious George lived in _____.
Africa   Florida   England

Curious George was always very _____.
unhappy   curious   hungry

Curious George saw a man with a _____ hat.
pink   orange   yellow

Name:

Circle the answer that best fits in the blank.

The man put Curious George in a _____.

box   bag   cage

Curious George fell overboard trying to _____.

run   fly   swim

The man told Curious George he was taking him to a big _____.

zoo   house   jungle

Curious George called the _____ when he played with the phone.

fire department   little old man   library

Name: _____

Circle *the answer that best fills in the blank.*

The fireman took Curious George to _____.

church   prison   school

Curious George saw big red, yellow and green _____.

birds   balls   balloons

The zoo was a _____ place for Curious George to live.

nice   bad   awful

Finish the picture to show how Curious George flew through the air.

Name:

Name:

Supplies

White construction paper
Toilet roll tube
   or 6 ounce juice can
Crayons
Brown tempera paint

Instructions

Copy the patterns below onto white construction paper. Paint the tube or juice can brown. While that is drying, color and cut out the monkey patterns. Glue to tube. If you choose to use a juice can, it can be used as a pencil holder.

First Favorites: *Volume 1*

Name:

In your best handwriting, copy the sentence below.

Curious George was a good little monkey who lived in Africa.

CAPS FOR SALE
by Esphyr Slobodkina

Name:

Circle the correct answer.

Where did the peddler carry his wares?
Back   Top of his head   Cart

What color cap did the peddler put on the top of his stack?
Red   Blue   Brown

For how much did the peddler sell his caps?
75¢   25¢   50¢

Who took the peddler's caps?
Monkeys   Little boys   A man

What did the hat thieves say when the peddler asked for his hats back?
Pst, pst, pst   Dum de dum dum   Tsz, tsz, tsz

What happened when the peddler threw his hat on the ground?
The monkeys laughed   The monkeys threw their hats on the ground   The monkeys sang

Name:

Color the caps below to match all the variety of hats the peddler sold.

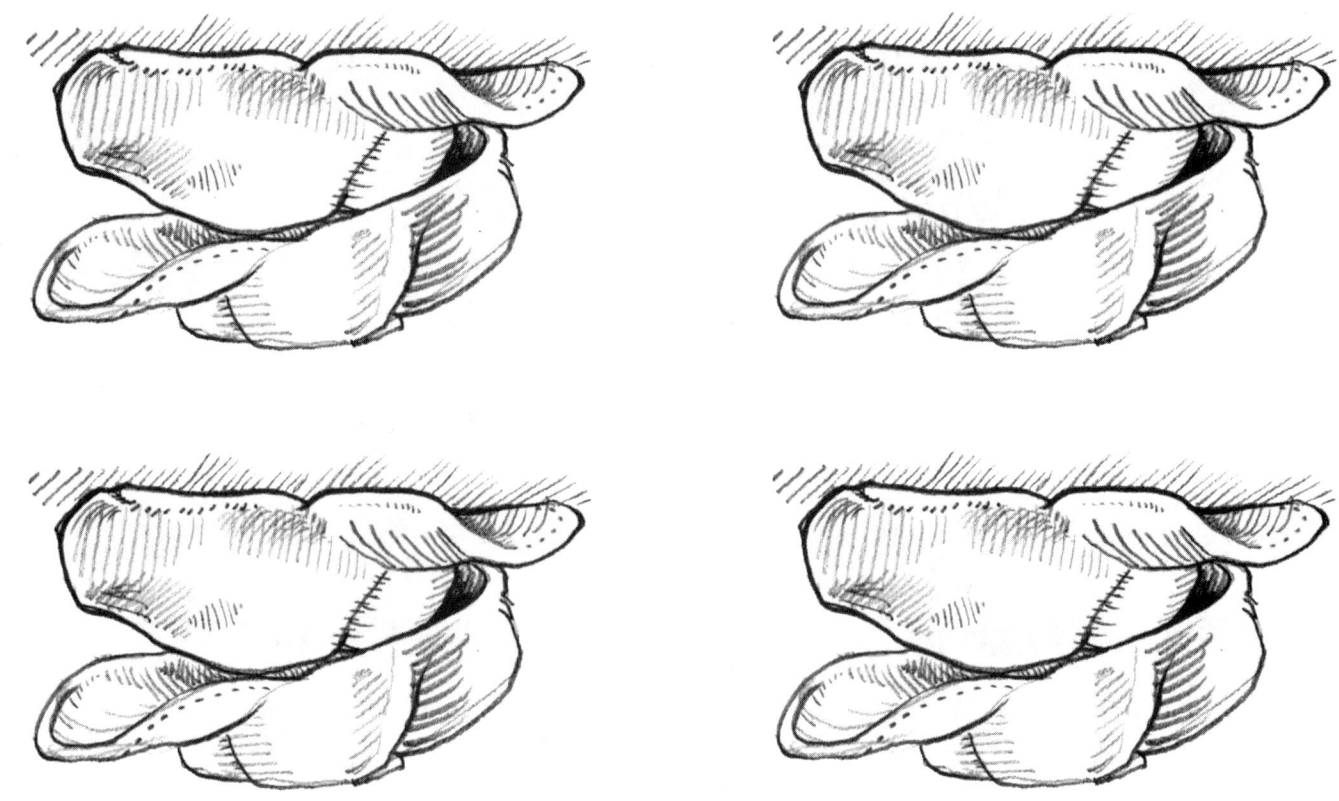

Name:

Follow the maze to get the monkey up into the middle of the tree.

21 | CAPS FOR SALE

First Favorites: *Volume 1*

Name:

In your best handwriting copy the sentence below.

Caps! Caps for sale! Fifty cents a cap!

Corduroy

by Don Freeman

Name:

Circle the correct answers.

Corduroy was a toy _____.
bear   cat   dog   turtle

Corduroy wore _____ overalls.
red   yellow   green   purple

Corduroy had lost a _____ on his overalls.
snap   button   pocket   patch

Corduroy thought that the _____ was a mountain.
escalator   table   refrigerator   chair

Name: _____

Circle the correct answers.

Corduroy went looking for a button. He thought he had found one on a _____.

chair   mattress   lamp   flashlight

A _____ came to take Corduroy home to be her very own.

little girl   little boy   Mommy   Grandmother

Corduroy told Lisa he had always wanted a _____.

fish   friend   bat   bed

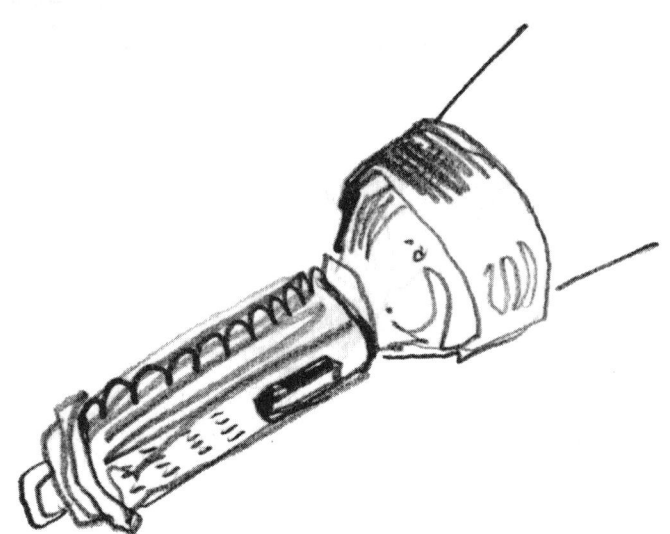

Name: _____

Correctly color in Corduroy and his overalls. Then cut them out and dress him.

27 | Corduroy

First Favorites: *Volume 1*

Name:

Draw a picture of your favorite stuffed animal. Write three sentences describing it.

My favorite stuffed animal is

Name: _____

In your best handwriting, copy the sentence below.

Corduroy is a bear who lived in the toy department of a big store.

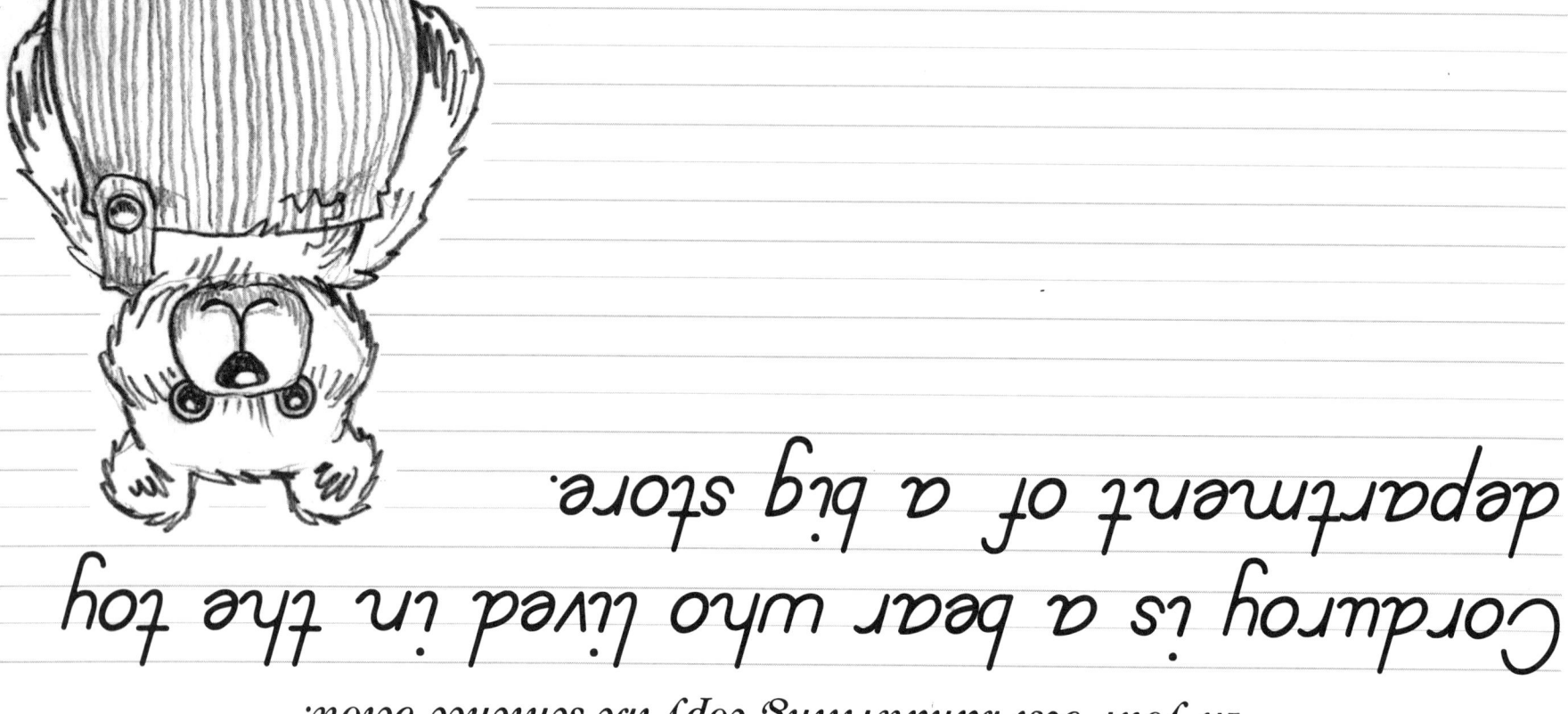

If You Give a Mouse a Cookie

by Laura Joffe Numeroff

Name:

Mouse Cookies *(Nice Rice Mice)*

Ingredients:

3 Tablespoons butter
1 pkg. (10 oz.) regular marshmallows
6 cups puffed rice cereal
Strawberry Licorice laces *(whiskers)*
Jujubes *(eyes)*
Cinnamon hearts *(nose)*
Vanilla icing *(glue)*
Graham cracker sticks *(broken in two for ears)*

Directions:

Melt butter and marshmallows, stirring to mix. Add cereal and stir until coated. Butter your hands to form cereal mixture into oblong shapes. Add candies to form eyes and nose. Insert Graham crackers and licorice for the ears and whiskers.

Name:

In your best handwriting copy the sentence below.

If you give a mouse a cookie, he's going to ask for a glass of milk.

Blueberries For Sal
by Robert McCloskey

Name: _____

Answer the questions below using complete sentences.

Why did Little Sal and her mother need to bring their pails to Blueberry Hill?

What sound did Little Sal hear when she dropped the blueberries into her pail?

Name:

Answer the questions below using complete sentences.

Why did Little Sal not fill her pail of berries as fast as her mother?

What did Little Sal meet while picking berries?

Name: _____

Answer the question below using a complete sentence.

What did Little Bear meet while picking berries?

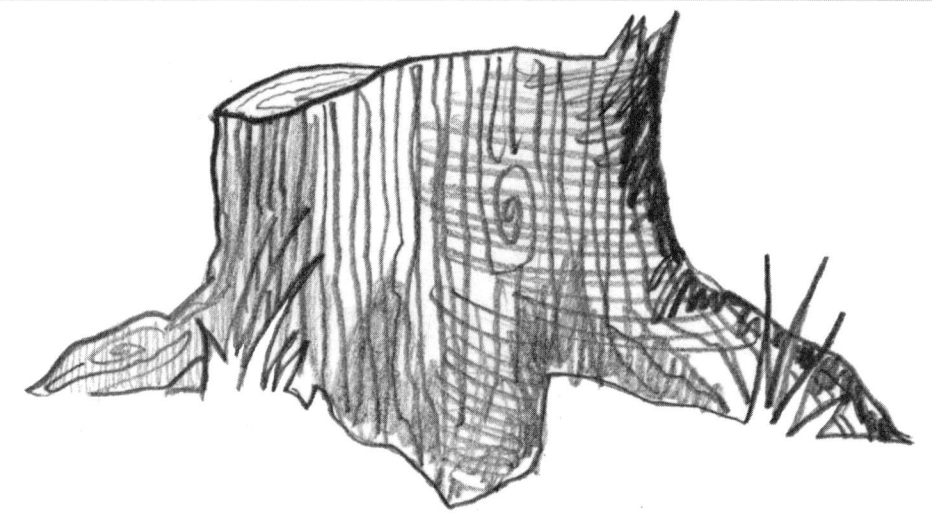

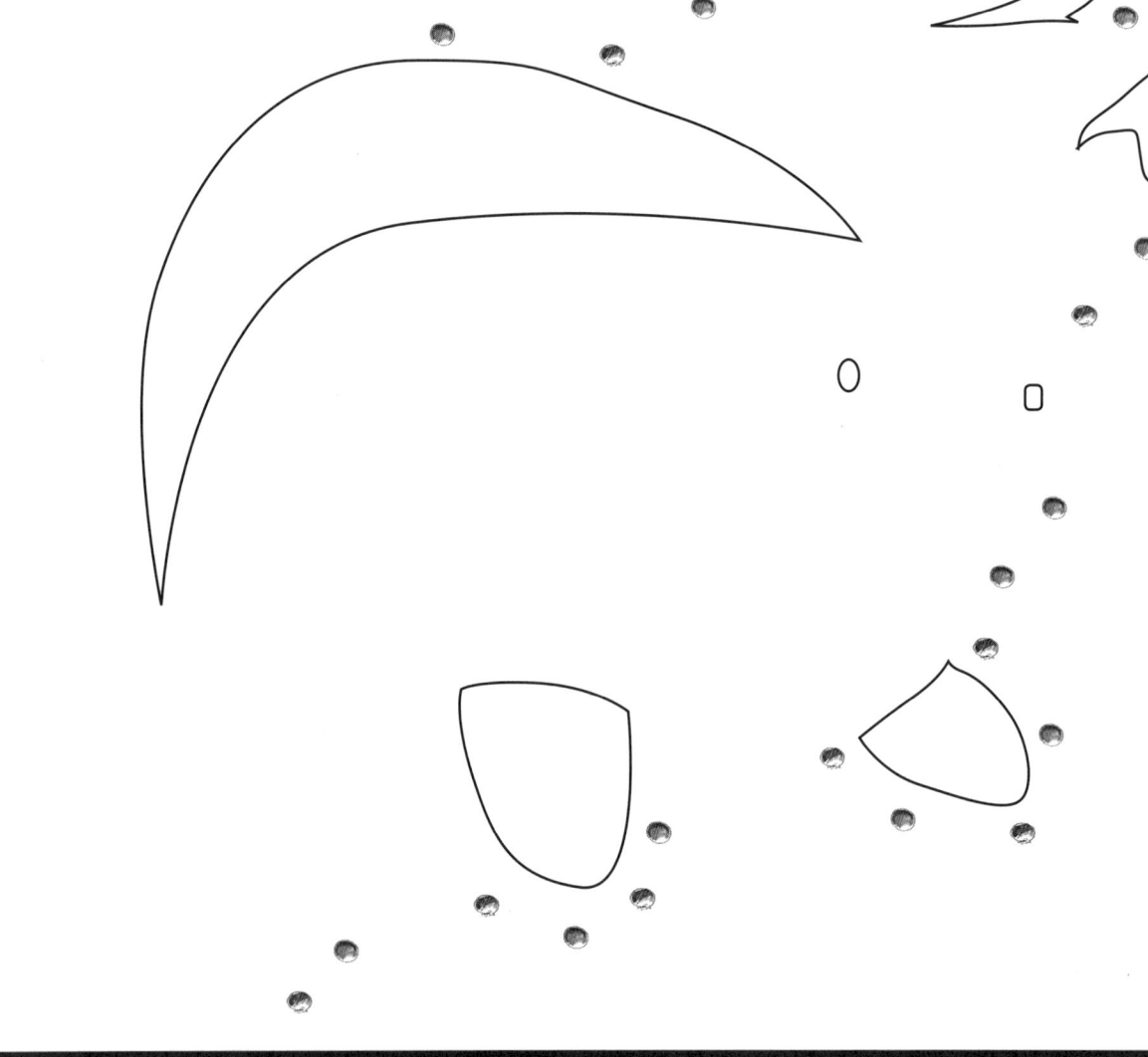

Name:

Connect the berries and color in the outlined areas to show who Sal met.

Name:

Cut out the boxes and glue them on another piece of paper in the correct order.

 Little Sal and Little Bear find their mothers	 Little Bear runs into Sal's mother	 Little Sal runs into Mother Bear
 Little Bear followed his mother as she walked through the bushes eating berries	 Little Sal and her mother go to Blueberry Hill to pick berries	 Little Sal and her mother can berries for the winter

Name:

In your best handwriting, copy the sentence below.

One day, Little Sal and her mother took their pails to Blueberry Hill to pick blueberries.

The Little Engine That Could
by Watty Piper

Name: _____

Fill in the blanks.

The little train said chug, chug, _____, puff, puff, _____, ding-dong, _____ as it rumbled over the tracks.

She was a _____ little train.

The train cars were filled full of good things for _____ and _____.

List six things that the train carried.

_____ _____

_____ _____

_____ _____

Name:

Fill in the blanks.

The little train puffed merrily along when all of a sudden she _____.

The Passenger Engine, the _____ Engine and the _____ Engine all refused to help pull the little train over the mountain.

The Little Blue Engine was only used for _____ trains in the yard.

The Little Blue Engine said, "I _____ I can, I _____ I can."

Name: _____

Match the words on the left to the definitions on the right by drawing a line.

rumble	bright, reflecting light
jolly	a room for entertaining visitors
jerk	to move with a deep, long, rolling sound
shiny	a bunk
berth	full of fun
parlor	tired, needing rest
dingy	to give a quick, sudden movement
weary	dirty or dark

Name:

In your best handwriting copy the sentence below.

I think I can, I think I can,

I think I can, I think I can.

Name:

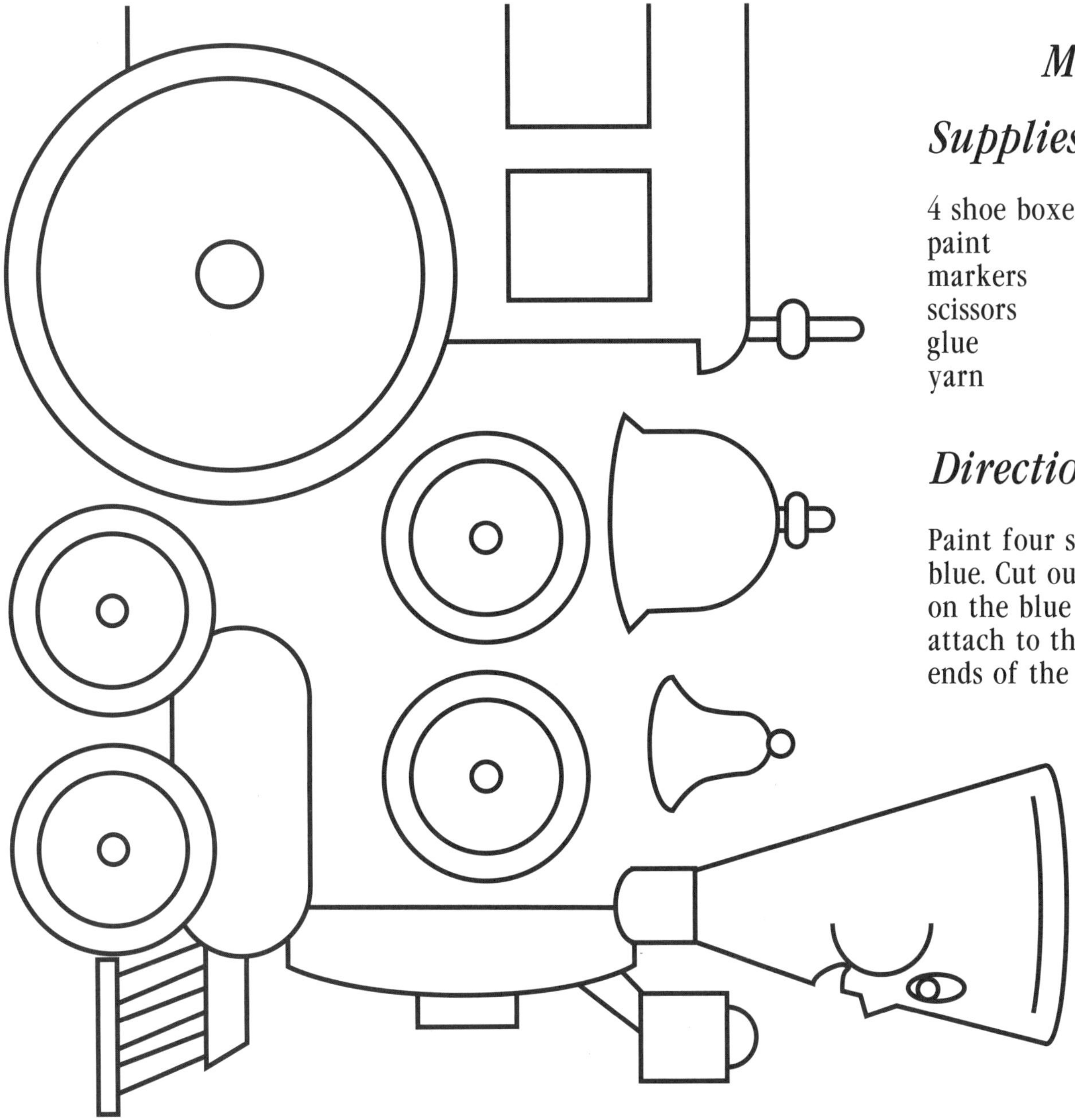

Make Your Own Train

Supplies:

4 shoe boxes
paint
markers
scissors
glue
yarn

Directions:

Paint four shoe boxes, making sure one is painted blue. Cut out the patterns for the engine and glue on the blue shoebox. Cut out the extra wheels and attach to the other shoeboxes. Poke holes in the ends of the shoe boxes and attach them with yarn.

Floss
by Kim Lewis

Name: _____

Answer the questions below by adding a word to make the sentences complete.

Who was Floss?
Floss was a Border _____.

What did Floss like to play?
Floss liked
to play _____.

Name: _____

Answer the questions below by adding a word to make the sentences complete.

Where did the Farmer take Floss?
The farmer took Floss to his son's farm
to learn how to herd _____.

What did Floss think about
while on the farm?
Floss thought about playing
with the children. _____

Name: _____

Cut out the picture of the sheep, color it, and glue it onto a paper bag with cottonballs to make a sheep handpuppet.

Example:

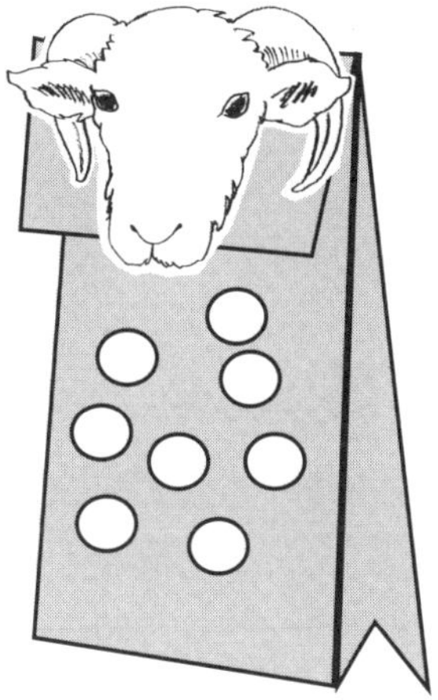

Name: _____

Cut out the picture of the dog, color it, and glue it onto a paper bag with cottonballs to make a dog handpuppet.

Name:

Draw a picture to show what happened to the sheep when Floss ran off with the children.

Name:

In your best handwriting copy the sentence below.

Floss was a young Border Collie who belonged to an old man in town.

A Chair for my Mother

by Vera B. Williams

Name:

Color in the pictures, then cut the boxes apart and glue them onto construction paper in the correct order as they appeared in the story.

Uncle Sandy gave me a quarter to put in our jar.

We moved into the house. The neighbors brought pizza, cake and ice cream.

The house was on fire. The sofa and all the chairs burned.

We went shopping in four furniture stores for a chair.

We set the chair beside the window. Now Moma sits down when she comes home from her job and I fall asleep in her lap.

My mother brought home paper wrappers and we wrapped all the nickles, dimes and quarters.

Color the chair to show what kind of chair you would like to buy. Then cut it out, wrap it around a 1 lb. 2 oz. peanut butter jar and glue large marshmellows under the flaps to make the armrests. Use the jar to store your coins!

Name:

Match the items on the left to those that go in on the right.

77 | A Chair for my Mother

First Favorites: *Volume 1*

Name: _____

Answer the question below using a complete sentence.

What did Mama want to put into the jar she brought home from the diner?

Name:

Answer the questions below using complete sentences.

Why did Mama not have a chair to sit in?

Who did Grandma call the kindest people?

Name: _____

Answer the questions below using complete sentences.

Why did Mother bring home paper wrappers?

Who sits in the chair?

Name:

In your best handwriting, copy the sentence below.

Mama brought home the biggest jar she could find at the diner for us to save all our coins to buy a chair.

HARRY

THE DIRTY DOG
by Gene Zion

Name:

Answer the questions below using complete sentences.

Who was Harry?

What did Harry not like to do?

Name:

Answer the questions below using complete sentences.

What did Harry bury in the back yard?

How did Harry get so dirty?

Name: _____

Answer the questions below using complete sentences.

When Harry came home what did his family think?

How did Harry finally convince his family he was home?

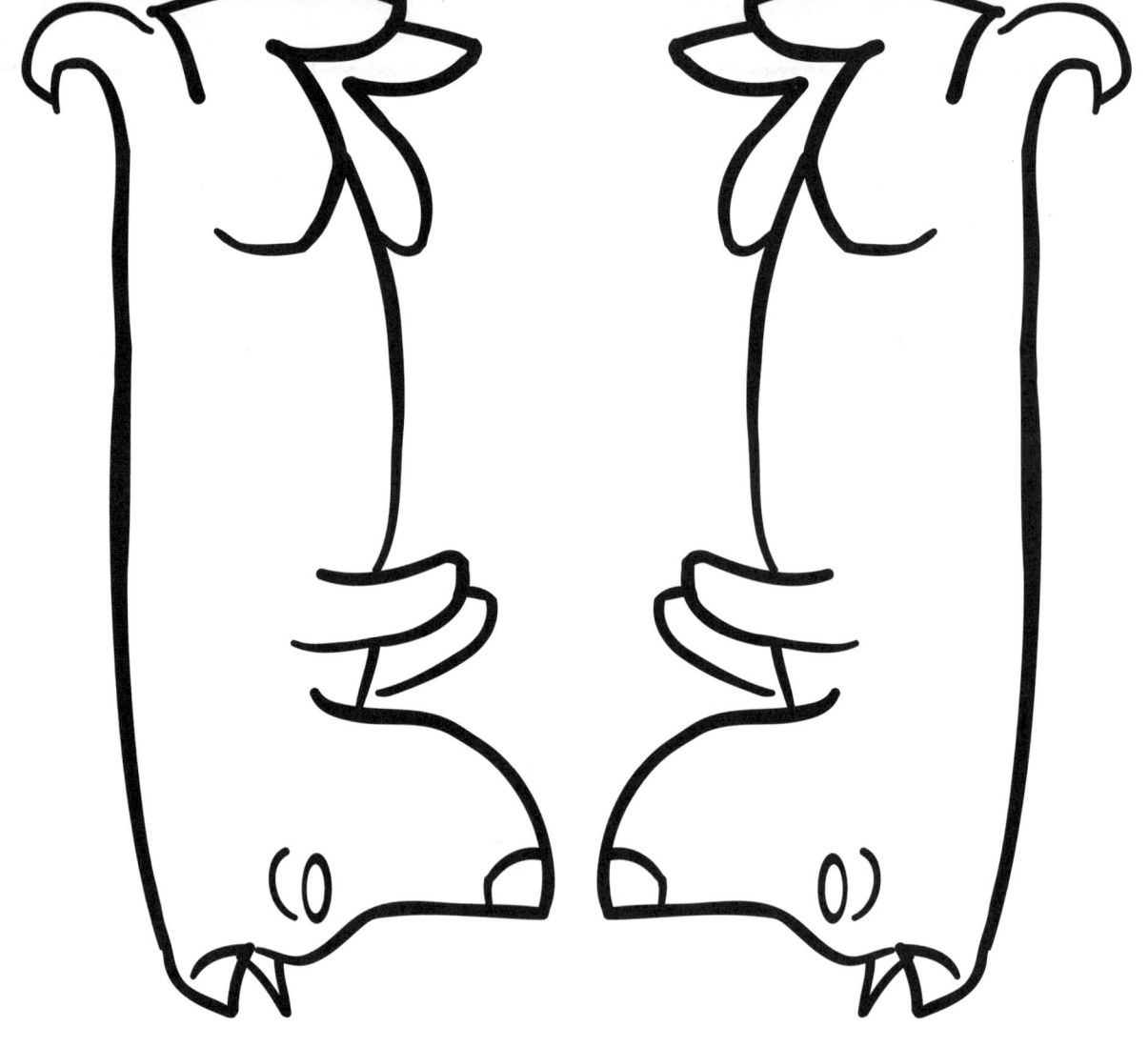

Color the picture of Harry

Before Harry Ran Away   After Harry Ran Away

Name:

Name:

In your best handwriting, copy the sentence below.

Harry was a little white dog with black spots, who loved everything except getting a bath.

Billy and Blaze

by C.W. Anderson

Name:

Answer the questions below using complete sentences.

What did Billy love more than anything else in the world?

What did Billy receive for his birthday?

Name: _____

Answer the questions below using complete sentences.

What color was the pony's nose?

Why did Billy name his pony Blaze?

Name:

What did Billy and Blaze find one day in the woods?

What did Billy name his dog?

Draw a picture of your favorite thing that Billy, Blaze and Rex did together.

Name:

*A noun is a word that is a person, place or thing.
An adjective is a word that describes something.
In each sentence below underline the nouns and circle the adjectives.*

And there stood a beautiful bay pony with four white feet and a white nose.

Then the judge pinned a blue ribbon on Blaze's bridle with First Prize printed in gold letters on it.

Billy set the silver cup in his room.

Using the frame provided, draw a horse like Blaze.

Name: _____

Name: _____

In your best handwriting, copy the sentence below.

Billy was a little boy who loved horses more than anything else in the world.

Bread and Jam for Frances
by Russell Hoban

Name: _____

Answer the questions below using complete sentences.

Why did Frances not like eating eggs?

What did Frances like to eat?

What did Frances think about jam?

Name:

Answer the questions below using complete sentences.

What did Frances do while she waited for the bus?

Why did Frances' mother and father just give her bread and jam?

Name: _____

Circle TRUE *if this happened in the story and* FALSE *if it did not.*

JAM	Frances loved to eat soft boiled eggs. TRUE | FALSE	Frances had two brothers and one sister. TRUE | FALSE
Gloria was Frances' baby sister. TRUE | FALSE	Frances loved to eat bread and jam. TRUE | FALSE	Frances did not like to eat new things. TRUE | FALSE
Frances sang as she waited for the bus. TRUE | FALSE	Frances was a horse. TRUE | FALSE	Albert only wanted to eat bread and jam. TRUE | FALSE
Frances' parents made her eat all the food on her plate. TRUE | FALSE	Frances' father loved spaghetti and meatballs. TRUE | FALSE	Frances got tired of eating only bread and jam. TRUE | FALSE

Name:

Color the food that Frances did not like to eat.

- bread
- eggs
- string beans
- spaghetti
- jam
- chicken salad
- veal

Name: _____

My favorite food is _____.
I like it because

Name:

In your best handwriting copy the sentence below.

Jam on biscuits, jam on toast, jam is the thing that I like most! Jam is sticky, jam is sweet, jam is tasty, jam is a treat.

Name: _____

Cut out the illustration on this page and attach to a paper plate. Cut holes for the eyes and smaller holes at the edges of the plate to tie string through.

WARNING: This mask will NOT enjoy jam as Frances does.

109 | Bread and Jam for Frances

First Favorites: *Volume 1*

Doctor DeSoto

by William Steig

Name:

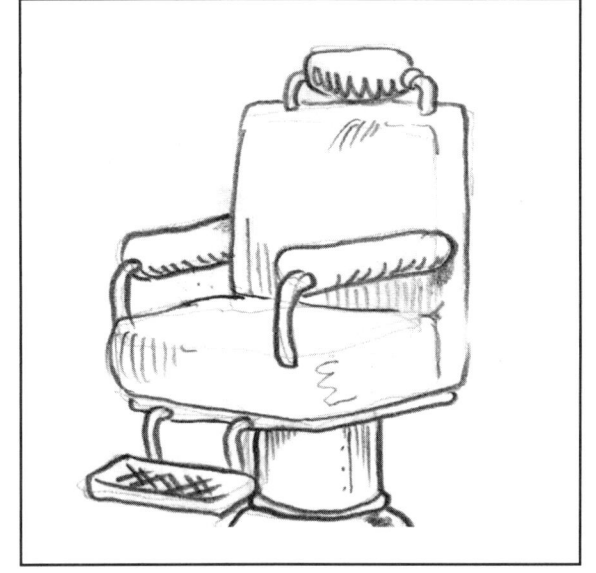

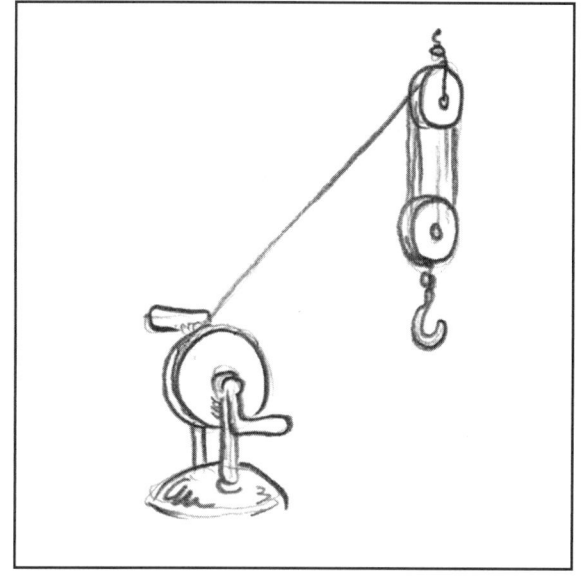

horse

hamster

elephant

pig

dog

cow

Doctor DeSoto treated all different sizes of patients.

Cut out the animals and paste them in their correct treatment place.

mole

gerbil

Name: _____

Draw a picture to illustrate what the fox was dreaming about.

Name: _____

Using a dictionary is fun! The words are in alphabetical order. Look up in a dictionary the words below and match the word to its correct definition.

hoist   easily frightened; shy

delicate   dizzy, faint

timid   to feel pain or distress

suffer   a small piece of food

misery   to lift or haul

morsel   to shake, tremble

quiver   very fine

woozy   suffering; distress

Name: _____

Cut out each sentence and place them in the order they occurred in the story.

Dr. DeSoto extracted the Fox's bad tooth.

The fox begged Dr. DeSoto to treat him.

The fox sat on the floor and removed his bandages.

Dr. DeSoto gave the fox a new tooth.

The fox was unable to open his mouth.

Name: _____

Copy the sentence below then draw a picture of some patients Dr. DeSoto treated.

Doctor DeSoto was a dentist who treated all kinds of patients.

Name:

Fill in the correct digraph: oo / ea / au / aw

Dr. DeSoto, the dentist did g___d work. The fox said, "How I love them r___with a pinch of salt and a...dry...white wine."

The fox loved his new t___th. The fox had made up his mind to ___t Dr. DeSoto and his wife. Dr. DeSoto told the fox to close his j___ tight.

Name:

Answer the questions below using complete sentences.

What kind of animals did Dr. DeSoto refuse to treat?

How did Dr. DeSoto outfox the fox?

Name:

Complete the idea below using complete sentences.

I just thought of a great use for dental floss, let me tell you about it...

Name: _____

In your best handwriting, copy the sentence below.

Doctor DeSoto was a compassionate and clever mouse-dentist.

Frog and Toad are Friends

Frog and Toad All Year

by Arnold Lobel

Name:

Circle TRUE *if the statement is true and* FALSE *if it is not.*

Frog went to Toad's house to tell him that it was Spring. — TRUE | FALSE

Toad was so excited to hear it was Spring that he leaped out of bed. — TRUE | FALSE

Frog explained to Toad that they could skip through the meadows, run through the woods and swim in the river. — TRUE | FALSE

Toad went back into the house and said come back and wake me up at half past May. — TRUE | FALSE

Frog tore the months of November, December, January, February, March, and April off of Toad's calendar. — TRUE | FALSE

Toad looked at the calendar and said, "It's not May, you are trying to trick me." — TRUE | FALSE

Name:

Frogs and Toads are similar in many ways, but different in others. Go to the library and find a book or two that will help you find out about frogs and toads and write your discoveries below.

FROGS

Color:
_____

Size:
_____

Where They Live:
_____

What They Eat:
_____

Distinguishing Features:
_____

Unusual Fact:
_____

TOADS

Color:
_____

Size:
_____

Where They Live:
_____

What They Eat:
_____

Distinguishing Features:
_____

Unusual Fact:
_____

Name: _____

Draw a picture in each box to illustrate what Toad did as he tried to think of a story to tell Frog. Make sure you put them in their correct order.

Name: _____

Summarize the events in "A Lost Button"

Name:

Button Hunt

Gather all kinds of old buttons making sure you have one button that is white, four-holed, big, round and thick. Hide all the buttons in the room (in the classroom setting, about twenty buttons will be needed per child). After reading the story, send the children on a "Button Hunt" to find Frog's lost button. A prize may be given to the one who finds the white, four-holed, big, round and thick button. Then allow the children to use all the buttons they collected to make a collage using glue on construction paper.

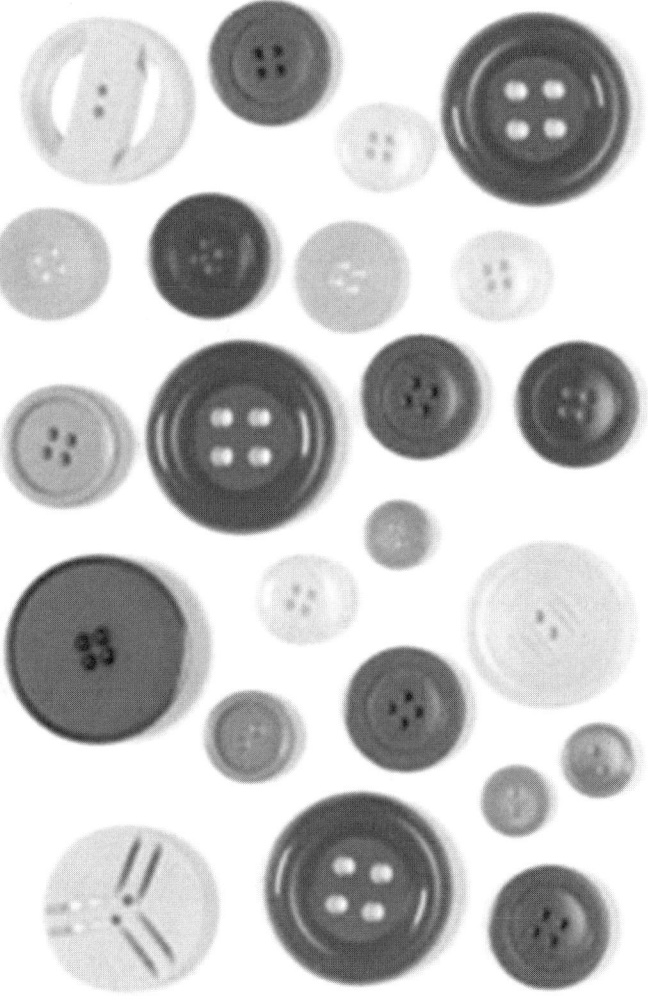

Name:

Describe Toad as he arrived at the pond.

Name:

Draw pictures and label all of the animals that laughed at Toad in his bathing suit.

Name: _____

Answer the questions below using complete sentences.

Why was Toad looking sad?

_____

_____

_____

_____

What did Frog do to cheer up Toad?

_____

_____

_____

_____

Name:

Answer the questions below using complete sentences.

How did Frog send the letter to Toad?

How long did it take for Toad to get Frog's letter?

Name:

Fill in the blanks.

List the clothes Frog gave Toad for winter.

_____

_____

_____

_____

A _____ told Toad that he was all alone on the sled.

Frog got scared and ran into a _____, then hit a _____ and dived into the _____.

Toad said, "Winter may be beautiful, but _____ is much better."

Frog took Toad on a _____ ride.

There was a bump and _____ fell off the sled.

Name:

Spring is just around the corner, but there are so many corners!

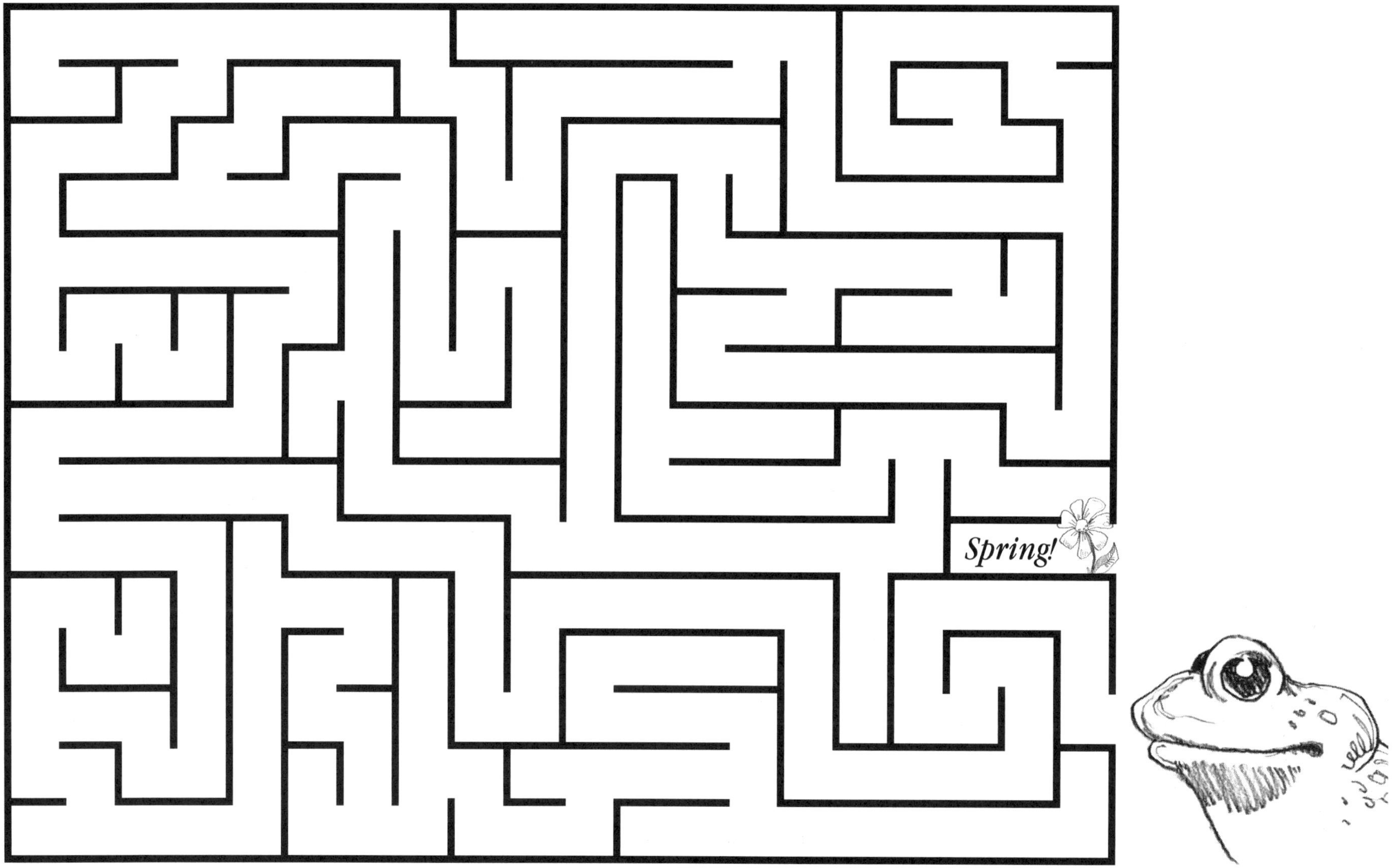

137 | Frog and Toad are Friends: The Corner

First Favorites: *Volume 1*

Name: _____

Answer the questions below using complete sentences.

What flavor ice cream did Toad buy at the store?

What happened to Toad on his way back with the ice cream?

Name:

Answer the question below using a complete sentence.

Did Frog and Toad ever get to eat ice cream together?

Name:

Read the story of The Surprise and make this autumn tree. You may want to photocopy this page onto thicker paper. Use orange, red, yellow and brown poster paints or stamp pads. Have the student press a finger tip or thumb tip into the color and then make a print on the tree to create the leaves.

Name:

Draw a line to match what Toad was going to use to help Frog.

What if Frog had fallen into a deep hole?   *Frying Pan*

What if Frog is lost in the woods?   *Rope*

What if Frog is being chased by a big animal?   *Lantern*

Name:

In your best handwriting copy the sentence below.

That night Frog and Toad were both
happy when they each turned out the
light and went to bed.

Name:

Using a shoebox, make a mantle clock like Frog gave Toad.

Directions:
Paint the shoebox brown and color the extra piece on this page. Glue in place to form the clock. Use a brass folding brad to attach the hands to the face.

First Favorites Comprehension Guide

Answers

Curious George

Pg. 9
monkey
Africa
curious
yellow

Pg. 10
bag
fly
zoo
fire department

Pg. 11
prison
balloons
nice

Pg. 12
The children should finish the picture of George by showing him flying through the air holding on to balloons.

Caps for Sale

Pg. 19
Top of his head
Red
50 cents
monkeys
tsz, tsz, tsz
The monkeys threw their hats on the ground.

Pg. 20
Gray, brown, blue, red

Pg. 21
Finish the maze.

Corduroy

Pg. 25
Bear
Green
Button
Escalator

Pg. 26
Mattress
Little girl
friend

Pg. 28
The overalls should be colored green.

If You Give a Mouse a Cookie

Pg. 33
Name some things asked for by the mouse.
They should have three from the following list:
Glass of milk
A straw
A napkin
A mirror
A pair of nail scissors
A broom
To read him a story
To see the pictures
Paper and crayons
Pen
Scotch tape

Why did the mouse want a mirror?
To make sure he doesn't have a milk mustache.

Pg. 34
Why did the mouse want a pair of nail scissors?
To trim his hair.

What will the mouse need if he wants to take a nap?
A box with a blanket and a pillow.

Pg. 35
cookie
milk
straw
napkin
mirror
mustache
mirror
hair
scissors
trim
broom
sweeping
room
floors

Pg. 36
nap
box
blanket
pillow
story
books
pictures
pictures
paper
crayons
picture
picture
name
pen

Pg. 37
refrigerator
scotch tape
drawing
refrigerator
thirsty
milk
milk
cookie

Pg. 38
Any picture is acceptable

First Favorites Comprehension Guide

Answers

Pg. 39
The child should write three sentences that describes a particular kind of cookie. You may need to help younger children by writing down what they verbally and allowing them to copy it.

Pg. 40
Color: brown, black or white
Size: 2 inches
Favorite feature: could be beady eyes, cute pink nose, etc
Tail length: 2 inches

Blueberries for Sal

Pg. 45
Why did Little Sal and her mother need to bring their pails to Blueberry Hill?
To carry the blueberries they picked home.
What sound did Little Sal bear when she dropped the blueberries into her pail?
Kuplink, kuplank, kuplunk

Pg. 46
Why did Little Sal not fill her pail of berries as fast as her mother?
Because she ate most of the ones she picked.
What did Little Sal meet while picking berries?
A mother crow and her children and Little Bear's mother

Pg. 47
What did Little Bear meet while picking berries?
A mother partridge and her children and Sal's mother

Pg. 48
*Little Sal and her mother go to Blueberry Hill to pick berries
Little Bear followed his mother as she walked through the bushes eating berries
Little Sal runs into Mother Bear
Little Bear runs into Sal's mother
Little Sal and Little Bear find their mothers
Little Sal and her mother can berries for the winter*

Pg. 50
Connecting the dots will form a bear.

The Little Engine That Could

Pg. 55
Chug
Puff
Ding-dong
Happy
Boys, girls
Toy animals, giraffes, teddy bears, baby elephant, dolls, toy clown, toy engines, airplanes, tops, jack-knives, picture puzzles, books, oranges, apples, milk, spinach, peppermint drops, lollypops, after-meal treats *(should have six from the list)*

Pg. 56
Stopped
Freight
Rusty old
Switching
Think
Think

Pg. 59
Rumble: to move with a deep, long, rolling sound
Jolly: full of fun
Jerk: to give a quick, sudden movement
Shiny: bright, reflecting light

Berth: a bunk
Parlor: a room for entertaining visitors
Dingy: dirty or dark
Weary: tired, needing rest

Floss

Pg. 63
Collie
ball

Pg. 64
sheep
ball

Pg. 65
should show a picture of sheep running away; into the garden and into the road.

A Chair for My Mother

Pg. 73
3/2/1/5/6/4

Pg. 77
jar: coins
chair: mother
house: fire
shoes: feet
truck: chair

Pg. 78
What did Mama want to put into the jar she brought home from the diner?
coins

Pg. 79
Why did Mama not have a chair to sit in?
Because the old chair was burned up
Who did Grandma call the kindest people?
The people who brought them things

First Favorites Comprehension Guide

Answers

Pg. 80
Why did Mother bring home paper wrappers?
To wrap the coins to take them to the bank
Who sits in the chair?
All three of them

Harry the Dirty Dog

Pg. 85
Who was Harry?
A white dog with black spots.
What did Harry not like to do?
Get a bath.

Pg. 86
What did Harry bury in the back yard?
The scrubbing brush
How did Harry get so dirty?
Running away from home.

Pg. 87
When Harry came home what did his family think?
That there was a strange dog in the back yard.
How did Harry finally convince his family he was home?
He got a bath and washed the dirt off.

Pg. 88
Before Harry ran away: a white dog with black spots
After Harry ran away: a black dog with white spots

Billy and Blaze

Pg. 93
What did Billy love more than anything in the world?
Horses
What did Billy receive for his birthday?
A beautiful bay pony

Pg. 94
What color was the pony's nose?
White
Why did Billy name his pony Blaze?
Because he had a white blaze down his face

Pg. 95
What did Billy and Blaze find one day in the woods?
A dog
What did Billy name his dog?
Rex

Pg. 96
Anything from the book acceptable

Pg. 97
And there stood a beautiful bay pony with four white feet and a white nose.
Then the judge pinned a blue ribbon on Blaze's bridle with First Prize printed in gold letters on it.
Billy set the silver cup in his room.

Bread and Jam for Frances

Pg. 103
Why did Frances not like eating eggs?
Because of the way they slide, their soft insides
What did Frances like to eat?
Bread and jam
What did Frances think about jam?
It was sticky, sweet and a treat

Pg. 104
What did Frances do while she waited on the bus?
She skipped and sang.
Why did Frances' mother and father just give her bread and jam?
So that she would get tired of it.

Pg. 105
Frances loved to eat soft boiled eggs/false
Frances had two brothers and one sister/false
Gloria was Frances' baby sister/true
Frances loved to eat bread and jam/true
Frances did not like to eat new things/true
Frances sang as she waited for the bus/true
Frances was a horse/false
Albert only wanted to eat bread and jam/false
Frances' parents made her eat all the food on her plate/false
Frances' father loved spaghetti and meatballs/true
Frances got tired of eating only bread and jam/true

Pg. 106
Color the veal, string beans, eggs, chicken salad, spaghetti

Pg. 107
The children should fill in their favorite food and then answer the question I like it because....

Doctor DeSoto

Pg. 113
Dentist chair: hamster, gerbil, mole
Ladder: pig, dog
Hoist: elephant, horse, cow

Pg. 115
The children should draw a picture of the fox dreaming of eating a mouse.

First Favorites Comprehension Guide

Answers

Pg. 116
hoist: to lift or haul
delicate: very fine
timid: easily frightened; shy
suffer: to feel pain or distress
misery: suffering; distress
morsel: a small piece of food
quiver: to shake
woozy: dizzy; faint

Pg. 117
The fox begged Dr. DeSoto to treat him.
The fox sat on the floor and removed his bandages.
Dr. DeSoto extracted the fox's bad tooth.
Dr. DeSoto gave the fox a new tooth.
The fox was unable to open his mouth.

Pg. 120
good
raw
tooth
eat
jaws

Pg. 121
Animals that were dangerous to mice.
He glued the fox's jaws together.

Pg. 127
Frog went to Toad's house to tell him that it was Spring. True
Toad was so excited to hear it was Spring that he leaped out of bed. False
Frog explained to Toad that they could skip through the meadows, run through the woods and swim in the river. True
Toad went back into the house and said come back and wake me up at half past May. True
Frog tore the months of November, December, January, February, March, and April off of Toad's calendar. True
Toad looked at the calendar and said, "It's not May, you are trying to trick me." False

Pg. 128
Toad walked up and down the porch.
He stood on his head.
He poured water on his head.
He banged his head against the wall.

Pg. 131
He did not want anyone to see him in his bathing suit.

Pg. 132
Be sure the following animals are included:
turtle, lizards, snake, field mouse and Frog.

Pg. 133
Because he never got any mail. He wrote him a letter.

Pg. 134
He gave it to the snail to deliver. Four days.

Pg. 135
coat, snowpants, hat, scarf
sled
Frog
crow
tree
rock
snow
bed

Pg. 137
chocolate
The ice cream melted all over him.

Pg. 138
Yes, they went back to the store and ate their ice cream cones in the shade.

Pg. 140
deep hole: rope
lost in woods: lantern
chased by animal: frying pan